# Questions and Answers—

# The Life of Marcus Mosiah Garvey

A BIOGRAPHICAL PROFILE

By

## LEONARD FRANKLIN MORRIS
*Impressionist, Portraitist, Muralist,*
*Multi-Faceted Composition Specialist*

ISBN: 1-4033-8280-8 (e-book)
ISBN: 1-4033-8281-6 (Paperback)

Library of Congress Control Number:  2002095435

This book is printed on acid free paper.

Printed in the United States of America
Bloomington, IN

1stBooks - rev. 01/21/03

# INTRODUCTION

This book may not fulfill everything. It may not cover all the questions and answers, but it is about what it is like to be a Negro in a land where they kept the Negro down.

Here is a great Jamaican in the twentieth century, a forceful leader who worked hard to develop a spirit of pride among his people particularly American Negroes. He turned their attention to the birthplace of their foreparents – Africa. He changed many negative attitudes they had about themselves.

Marcus Garvey was born in the parish of St. Ann, Jamaica, West Indies, in 1887. He learned the printing trade at an early age and became a foreman in a printing plant in Kingston, Jamaica. He also worked at one time in the Government Printing Office.

Marcus Garvey was always concerned about race problems thus he had other interests besides printing. He realized that black people needed a new spirit. He started to concentrate and devote himself to help his brother and sisters. He founded the Universal Negro Improvement Association. Mr. Garvey then went to England and studied about Africa at London University.

In 1916, Garvey came to the United States, where he founded a back to Africa movement. His plan was to develop Africa as a home for Negroes throughout the world. Marcus Garvey was an eloquent speaker. His followers listened intensively. The back to Africa plan offered American Negroes a new vision. It gave them a place where they could rule themselves. It offered them an escape from the poverty and oppression they faced in the world, particularly in America.

By 1923, Garvey claimed to have six million followers. In 1929 he founded the Black Star Steamship Line to provide transportation to Africa. He started the Negro Factory Corporation, the Black Cross Nurses, and the newspaper, *The Negro World*, but the Back to Africa Movement failed because most Negroes did not fully understand the movement and considered America their home. They did not want to leave the country they had helped to build.

Unfortunately, the plan did not receive the full support from the majority of the black African nations. And, at the same time, the expenses of all his plans began to burden him. He lost all the monies he collected. His dreams faded, he was black-mailed, and arrested for mail fraud. After two years in the Tombs prison in New York City, he was deported. Before he went to jail, Garvey gave an impassioned address to the jury: "Gentlemen, will you let the tiger loose?" Sad to say, he died in London, poor and lonely.

Most American Negro leaders of the 1920s did not support the ideas of Marcus Garvey. They felt he had weakened their fight for equal rights throughout the world. How wrong they were! Today, however, Marcus Garvey is respected for his beliefs. He gave American Negroes a feeling of self respect, which many had never felt before.

In this book I have presented my paintings that include images of Marcus Garvey and of my feelings about his thoughts and beliefs.

**Leonard Franklin Morris**


For Marcus Mosiah Garvey, "The Thoughtful Negro... looks to... cultural and intellectual development of the race as the only hope through which a new civilization can be projected and a new concept become evident."

What is not generally recognized is that Marcus Garvey – poet, philosopher, dramatist, essayist, elocutionist, and public lecturer was also a champion, patron, and performer of the arts. His poem, an allegory, "A Night in Hell", was performed in a variety program at the Ward Theatre in Kingston, Jamaica in 1922, and his epic "The Tragedy of White Injustice" while making allusions to the standard works of English Literature, at the same time inveighs against social injustice. His dialogues from the "Black Man" were published in the 1930's, and in "A Talk With Afro-West Indians" his use of classical allusions and influences convey his concepts of the greatness and nobility of the African.

Leonard Franklin Morris, internationally known, and practitioner of the visual arts, is the embodiment of the "Thoughtful Creator"

iv

Garvey so eloquently alluded to in his popular writings, the man who imagines through his creative visions and artistry, the transformation of the race to a higher intellectual and creative order. Morris remains the only artist who has attempted a visual chronicle of eighty works *"The Life and Times of the Late Jamaican National Hero, The Hon. Marcus Mosiah Garvey*, documenting in oil, watercolor, and pen sketches, Garvey's birth, the house in which he was born, his arrest by the FBI on a train at 125$^{th}$ street, and up to his death. For this, he is now known as the "Garvey Man".

"My work takes shape around images and ideas that focus on the Black experience" says Morris. "That is why I painted the Garvey series to symbolize the vast contributions that one man made to the race, and to keep his dream alive."

"Up you mighty race."

**Professor Horace A. Banbury**
City University of New York

# QUESTIONS AND ANSWERS

Q  Where was Garvey born, and when?

A  Garvey was born in the parish of St. Ann, Jamaica West Indies, on August 17, 1887.

Q  What tribe was he descended from:

A  He was a descendant of the Maroons.

Q  Who was Marcus Garvey's father and mother, what type of work did they do?

A  His father was Marcus Garvey, Sr.; his mother's name was Sarah. His father was a master mason. He did both stone and brick work beautifully, but he always acted as if he did not belong among the villagers. He was well read and acted as a local lawyer. He was silent, stern, and had the strength of an ox.

Q  How many sisters and brothers did Garvey have?

A  Marcus had nine brothers and one sister. The brothers died at an early age. He and his sister lived to maturity.

Q  What schools did he attend?

A  He attended the schools of his town and was graduated from the Church of England High School. In addition, he was tutored by the Rev. W. H. Solely, and Rev. P. A. Conahan. He eventually went to England and studied for eighteen months at Birkbeck College (attendance 1912 to 1913). His records at Birkbeck College, now a part of London University, unfortunately, were destroyed during the blitz of 1940. Some doubt whether he was a student or not.

Q  What faith did Marcus Garvey belong to?

A  Marcus Garvey belonged to the Roman Catholic faith and was a supporter of the African Orthodox Church.

Q   What was the population of Jamaica when Garvey was a child?

A   At the time of Garvey's birth, the population of Jamaica numbered just over 600,000. Negroes, 78 percent, and mixed bloods, or colored, about 20 percent.

Q   When was Garvey aware of racial differences of skin?

A   He became aware of racial differences when he was fourteen years old. A white girl (his neighbor) told him she was going away to Scotland to study and after saying goodbye, her parents told her that she must no longer see or write to him because he was a nigger.

Q   When did he start to work?

A   He started working at an early age because of family financial difficulties. He worked as an apprentice in the printing trade with his godfather, a Mr. Burrowes, at P. A. Benjamin Company, Kingston, Jamaica, West Indies.

Q   How was the progressing on his job?

A   He was elevated on his job as a master printer and foreman. Wages were very low so his co-workers asked him to speak for them concerning the matter. He had meetings on what to do, and he called for a strike, which was agreed on by the workers. Unfortunately, with all that effort he lost his claims and his job. He got a job at the Government Printing Office shortly after.

Q   When did Garvey first speak to a crowd?

A   Garvey's first attempt to speak to a crowd was in 1907 at the age of twenty. He was met with rude rebuffs and was bluntly told "country boy shut up your mouth"; it did not bother him, he continued to gain confidence.

Q   Why was he so concerned about lower-class blacks?

A   Garvey was very concerned about lower-class blacks, because of the unfairness and the injustice they endured and because many were afraid to speak out. They were living under restrictions, so he had to do something about it.

Q   What was his destiny for black people, and what was he trying to say to white society?

A   Garvey's motto was "One God, One Aim, One Destiny." "Let justice be done to all mankind, and blacks return to Africa to strengthen the race and build a Nation."

Q   Who was that great American friend who corresponded with him while he was still in Jamaica?

A   He had a great friend in America, Booker T. Washington, noted for his autobiography, who communicated with him.

Q   Who was that friend who assisted him, and was his strongest hope?

A   His good friend in the United States was Booker T. Washington, who helped Garvey financially and educationally, but before Garvey could complete his travel plans, his good friend died (1915). Booker T. Washington was his strongest hope for a sympathetic reception in America.

Q   In what year did he turn to the United States for support?

A   In 1915 Garvey began to turn his mind to the United States for support of his program in Jamaica.

Q   When did he first travel outside of Jamaica?

A   Garvey first travelled outside of Jamaica to Costa Rica, where he got a job as a timekeeper at the United Fruit Company in 1910. Next he visited Panama (Bocas-del-Toro), and then drifted on to Colon, Ecuador, Nicaragua, Honduras, Columbia, and Venezuela.

Q   What year did he arrive in the United States and who was the president at that time?

A   He arrived in Harlem, New York, March 12, 1916. Woodrow Wilson was president.

Q   What was the name of the organization he founded?

A   He founded the Universal Negro Improvement Association.

Q  How did he became responsible for the journals *Watchman* and *Our Own*?
A  He had experience in printing and he was a learned man. These publishing ventures began in 1910. His friend, Dr. Love, was publisher of the *Advocate*.

Q  What kind of organization was his?
A  It has been described as social, fraternal, humanitarian, charitable, and educational.

Q  In what year did he organize the Universal Negro Improvement Association?
A  It was established in 1917 in New York City.

Q  Who was the man who first introduced Garvey in New York?
A  His name was Mr. Hubert H. Harrison, a well-known Negro writer and lecturer. Mr. Harrison was chairman of the Liberty League, and presented Garvey on June 12, 1917.

Q  How many American Negroes had served in the armed forces as of 1918?
A  400,000.

Q  Which was the most successful paper that Garvey edited?
A  *The Negro World*, established in January 1918. Educators regarded it as the most remarkable journalistic venture ever attempted by a Negro in the United States.

Q  What was the U.N.I.A. anthem?
A  It was "Ethopia, Thou Land of Our Father."

Q  What was the color of the banner?
A  It was black, green, and crimson.

Q   When did the U.N.I.A. adopt its Declaration of the Rights of the Negro People?
A   August 13, 1920.

Q   When was the first convention in New York?
A   It began on Sunday, August 1, 1920.

Q   Where was the U.N.I.A. headquarters located?
A   It was located in Harlem, at Liberty Hall.

Q   How many shares were allowed for each member?
A   200.

Q   How many shares did Garvey hold?
A   Garvey and four of his associates were each listed as holding forty shares of capital stock (1919).

Q   In what year did he buy the auditorium in Harlem?
A   In 1929 Garvey's organizational activities had progressed far enough for him to purchase a large auditorium located at 114 West 138 Street in Harlem.

Q   How much cash did Garvey have in 1919?
A   Garvey had $6 million and had planned to collect one dollar from each Negro.

Q   In what year did they begin to spell "Negro" with a capital *N*?
A   In 1929 the New York State Board of Education ordered all schools in New York that they must teach the spelling of "Negro" with a capital *N*.

Q   In what year was the Black Starline Ship company founded?
A   1919.

Q  What was the Black Starline capitalized amount and shares of stocks?
A  The Black Starline was capitalized at $500,000, composed of 100,000 shares of stock with a par value of five dollars each.

Q  Who was the captain of the *Shadyside*?
A  His name was Captain Jacob Wise.

Q  Which freighter did Garvey buy?
A  The S.S. *Yarmouth*, rechristened S.S. *Federick Douglas Merchant Flag Ship* of the Black Star Line, was purchased at a cost of $165,000 in 1919; the ship was built in 1887.

Q  Which was the other ship Garvey bought?
A  Garvey's organization bought the S.S. *Shadyside* at a cost of $35,000.

Q  When and where was the first voyage of *Frederick Douglas*?
A  Late in November 1919, she sailed from the 135th Street Pier, Harlem, New York City.

Q  What was the estimated circulation of *The Negro World*?
A  *The Negro World* had circulate between 60,000 to 200,000 in 1920. It reached the mass of Negroes throughout the world.

Q  What was the price of the paper?
A  *The Negro World* sold for five cents in America and ten cents in foreign countries.

Q  Who was Garvey's greatest black opponent in America?
A  His name was W. E. B. DuBois, editor of *Crisis*. He urged American Negroes to stand shoulder to shoulder with the white man.

Q What were the years of heavy lynching of the Negroes in the South?

A From 1917 to 1919, there were about thirty-eight victims. The summer of 1919 was called "Red Summer."

Q What was the nickname given to Garvey?

A He was called another West Indian carpetbagger.

Q How many states did Garvey visit, pleading for Negroes?

A He visited thirty-eight states.

Q Who was the man whom Garvey employed as his messenger and who started to criticize Garvey?

A He was Duse Mohammed Ali, an Egyptian who wrote terrible things about Garvey in his own paper, *The Negro World*, concerning Laziness and general worthless character. Garvey fired him in 1913.

Q Who was the former employee who attacked Marcus Garvey in his office on 135th Street in Harlem, arguing about $25 owed to him?

A His name was George Tyler who drew a revolver and fired at Garvey grazing him on his forehead and narrowly missing his right eye. In fleeing, Tyler leapt to his death.

Q Why did Garvey visit the K.K.K.?

A In June 1922 Garvey went to see the Imperial Wizard of the K.K.K. telling them of his relations with the West Indies and of his back to Africa effort, which impressed the white listeners.

Q There was someone from the N.A.A.C.P. who toured the states, speaking out against Garvey. Who was he?

A He was William Pickens who denounced Garvey and his African program. Thousands of hand bills with "Garvey must go" were distributed.

Q Who were the three Africans who condemmed William Pickens's philosophy of Africa and Africans?

A In a letter to the *New York Times*, August 10, 1922, three Africans denounced William Pickens's views that Africa was a heathen land where life was not safe on account of cannibals.

Q Which royalty from Africa sent a message to the U.N.I.A. convention, which the *New York World* reported?

A The king and queen of Abyssinia sent a message delivered by H. H. Topakyn, Persian consul general, who represented Abyssinia in this country. The contents of the message, read at the convention August 29, 1922; were particularly pleasing to the delegates and the audience. Men threw up their hats and women their handkerchiefs. Marcus Garvey, usually the personification of dignity, led in the cheering. In closing the king and queen wished the organization all success and invited members of the association to Come back to "the homeland." Teachers, artists, mechanics, writers, musicians, and others were invited.

Q Who were the men took legal action against Marcus Garvey?

A The men were Harry H. Pace, president of the Pace Phonograph Company; Robert S. Abbott, editor and publishers for the *Chicago Defender*; John E. Nail, president of Nail and Parker Incorporated, real estate agents; Julia P. Coleman, president of Hair Vim Chemical Company; William Pickens, field secretary of the N.A.A.C.P.; Chandler Owen, co-editor of the *Messenger*; and Robert V. Harris, editor of the *New York News*. All were prominent Negroes. They sent a long letter dated January 15, 1923, to Harry M. Dougherty, United States Attorney General, Department of Justice, Washington, D.C. to enforce a law against Marcus Garvey on grounds of mail fraud. They closed the letter by stating: "We sense the imminent menace of this insidious movement, which cancer-like is gnawing at the peace and safety of civic harmony and interracial concord."

Q  What year did Garvey go to prison and how long did he stay?
A  Garvey went to prison on June 21, 1922, for five years and a find of $1,000. He spent three months in jail. After a bond of $15,000 was posted, he was released, pending appeal. The judge was Julian Mack.

Q  What happened to Harry M. Doughtery in 1926?
A  Dougherty was tried on charges of conspiracy to defraud the government in connection with the transfer of alien property. He too was tried before Judge Julian Mack. While he was United States Attorney General, he was notorious for his crooked, shady political dealings.

Q  Why did Garvey not apply for U.S. citizenship?
A  Garvey was up against prominent men, who did everything to malign him and smash every practical effort of his. Their actions weakened all his efforts. If he had been a U.S. citizen he would not have been deported.

Q  Did the Communists help?
A  The Communists were willing to back Garvey against the K.K.K. The Communists revealed their true intentions in the *Daily Worker*, August 9, 1924. Garvey did not show any interest in their appeal.

Q  Why did Garvey send professional men to Liberia?
A  He wanted to help build the country and have the U.N.I.A. headquarters move to Liberia. C. King, president of Liberia, authorized his minister, Edwin Barclay, Secretary of State, to forward a letter to the U.N.I.A. for approval. Garvey sent six professionals to Liberia to work and teach.

*Leonard Morris*

# THE POLITICAL ACTIVITIES OF MARCUS GARVEY IN JAMAICA
**by**
**AMY JACQUES GARVEY**

The year 1929 was an agonizing 365 days for Marcus Garvey in Jamaica. Subtle, silent, systematic efforts were made to crush him and destroy his movement, when he would not heed the overtures of agents sent to please with him (for his own good) to give up the fight to change the condition of the black masses.

In July of that year a default judgment of G. O. Marke, a former officer of the parent body in New York City, was taken up by J. H. Cargill, solicitor in Jamaica. The hearing was held before Sir Fiennes Barrett Lennard, Chief Justice, who gave judgment and ordered the sale of all the properties and assets of the parent body of U.N.I.A. incorporated and unincorporated, and also of the local branches in Jamaica. Despite the fact that an appeal was pending, everything was sold.

During the hearing, the chief justice fined Garvey twenty-five pounds (sterling) for not producing the books of the branch, which books Garvey did not have in his possession. The local U.N.I.A. won the appeal, and the government had to refund the branch the price paid for their Liberty Hall at the auction sale, which was below market value. But Garvey got nothing for all the assets of the various auxiliary units sold by order of the Chief Justice.

The Isaiah Morter case was going through the courts of Belize, British Honduras, and to England on appeal. Mr. Morter, a black, left his estate to the U.N.I.A. "for African redemption." The Colonial Office (through the local judiciary) said this was for "illegal purposes" and despite the thousands of pounds spent for barristers and court fees, the parent body and Garvey never got the legacy.

Garvey and the movement were stripped financially, but they held the sixty international convention in Jamaica, and delegates heralded from around the world, defiant that the spirit of Garveyism would prevail.

Feeling the mighty hand of imperalism clothed in legal authority, Garvey decided to form a political party. He and his colleagues named it "The People's Political Party." In 1929 they issued a manifesto.

In the subsequent municipal elections they won three seats; they won one in the Legislative Council. They decided to run twelve candidates, one for each parish, for the general elections to the Legislative Council. The following are the planks of their platform:

1. Representation to the Imperial Parliament for a longer modicum of self-government.
2. Protection of native labour.
3. A minimum wage for the labouring and working classes of the island.
4. A law to protect the working and labouring classes of the country by insurance against accident, sickness, and death, occurring during employment.
5. A law compelling the employment of not less than 60 percent of native labour in all industrial, agricultural, and commercial activities engaged in this island.
6. The expansion and improvement of urban areas without the encumbrance or restraint of private proprietorship.
7. An eight-hour working day throughout Jamaica.
8. A law to encourage the promotion of native industries.
9. Land reform.
10. A law to impeach and imprison judges who, with disregard for British justice and constitutional rights, deal unfairly.
11. A Jamaican university for polytechnic.
12. The establishment of a government high school in the capital town of each parish, for the supply of free secondary education. Attached to said high school, a night continuation school to facilitate those desiring to study at night, in order to advance their education.

13. A public library in the capital town of each parish.
14. A National Opera House, with an academy of music and art.
15. Prison reform.
16. The compulsory improvement of urban areas in which large profits are made by trusts, corporations, combines and companies.
17. The appointment of official court stenographers to take official notes of all court proceedings in the Supreme Court, Resident Magistrates Courts, and Petty Session Court of the island.
18. The creation of a legal aid department to render advice and protection to such persons who may not be able to have themselves properly represented and protected in the courts of law.
19. A law for imprisonment of any person who by duress or undue influence would force another person to vote in any public election against his will, because of obligation, employment, or otherwise.
20. The granting to the townships of Montego Bay and Port Antonio the corporation right of cities.
21. A law to empower the government to secure a loan of three million (or more) pounds from the imperial government, or otherwise, to be used by the government, under the management of a department of the director of agriculture in developing the crown lands of the island, agriculturally, and otherwise, with the object of supplying employment for our surplus unemployed population, and to find employment for stranded Jamaicans abroad, and that the government purchase such ships as are necessary from time to time, to facilitate the marketing of the produce gathered from these crown lands, and at the same time conveniently offering an opportunity to other producers to ship and market their produce.
22. The beautifying and of Kingston Race Course into a National Park, similar to Hyde Park in London.

23. The establishment by the government of an electrical system to supply cheap electricity to such growing and prospering centers as are necessary.
24. A law to establish clinical centers from which trained nurses are to be sent out to visit homes in rural districts, and to teach and demonstrate sanitary and better health methods in the care of home and family.
25. A law to empower the parochial board of each parish to undertake under the direction of the central government, the building of model sanitary homes for peasantry by the system of easy payments, to cover a period of ten to twenty years.
26. A law to prevent profiteering in the sale of land in urban and suburban areas to the detriment of the expansion of healthy home life for citizens of moderate means.

As leader of the party Garvey spoke at Cross Roads Square on September 10, 1929. A few days later he was arraigned in court on a second contempt charge, before the same chief justice and two other judges. The basis of the charge was the tenth plank of the manifesto. He was found guilty and sentenced to three months imprisonment, with a fine of one hundred pounds.

On release from prison he only had a couple of weeks to campaign, and without funds. Here are a few points me made:

Workers should be insured against sickness and accidents while employed... the earning capacity of the workers must be increased, which will benefit all classes of society. In this way workers will be able to spend more by earning more...

No encouragement is being given to the natives to foster and promote industries. The result is that Jamaica is grown up to be a country of consumers. Out of our by-products of agriculture we produce nothing. We import shoes, clothes, hats etc., when most of these things could be made right here.

Canning and tanning factories would be a great encouragement to the farmers in the country parishes, whose surplus fruits go to waste, and the skins of the animals bring little or nothing.

My opponents say I am against white and fair-skinned people. This is not so. I am against the class system here which keeps the poor man down, and the poor are mostly black people. It is only natural, therefore, that their interest should be nearest and dearest to my heart... Let us all work together as fellow Jamaicans, and bring in the changes for New Jamaica.

When the election returns were announced, Garvey was a shocked and grieved man. However, he went through the parishes and thanked those who had voted for his party. He said: "The voters have turned back the clock of progress for another ten years, but party system is well established in your minds, and it will come, it is bound to come."

In a letter dated February 1, 1930, reprinted in the *Negro World*, Wesley Atherton commented on the campaign:

Rum and human depravity blocked the path of Marcus Garvey. The terrible reverse which he received at the polls was due in no sense whatever to lack of organization. With the limited means at his command, his campaign could not have been better organized. He has lost in what was almost a rum war, a money scramble. With the bait dangling before their gaze, the red linen of filthy lucre, Negro Sons of African slaves, in this enlightened age voted away their birthright, and suffered themselves to be indentured for another five years under conditions that has sucked their vitals to the very bone. They traded on the future happiness of their children, and trampled their manhood into the dust. With the whip of the slave master still cracking in their ears, they followed the stream of molten gold down the hills of St. Andrew to vote against Marcus Garvey.

They stabbed him fiercely in the back, and while now recovering from that burtal wound, he stands before the bar of public opinion, facing the charges of his traducer. Those who can, must help, and those of us who cannot, must weep.

But the mournful dirge of the People's Political Party, not Garveyism, will not be sung in his generation, nor in the next, it shall synchronize only with the passage of time into eternity, both causes are immortal, and must survive all human, material barriers and impositions. Marcus Garvey has secured a wider niche in the hall of fame.

In October 1929, Garvey was elected to the Kingston and St. Andrew Corporation Council, but having to serve three months in prison on the second contempt charge, he was unable to take the oath and function as a councillor. He applied for leave; it was denied by a majority of one, but the lawyer for the corporation ruled that it was discretionary. Garvey took his seat on release from prison, then some of the councillors maneuvred again to unseat him, but they finally lost out.

Arising out of the underhand tatics used to keep him out of the council, an article was written in *The Blackman* in which it stated in part: "The corporation is entirely opposed to the welfare of the country... The government is also bereft of common decency, not to diginity, and common sense. It is true our faith in the local administration of affairs is sorely tired; perhaps we should not be, but our confidence in British fairplay is not upheld by the manifestation we behold day by day..."

Garvey, T. Aikman, editor, and Coleman Beecher, circulating manager, were brought before the court for seditious libel. Although Aikman admitted writing the editorial in question, and Garvey did not see it, as he was traveling in the parishes, the same chief justice acquitted Beecher. He reffered to Aikman "as the tool of Garvey," and sentenced him to three months imprisonment. Garvey, he said, was criminally responsible, and sentenced him to six months imprisonment. Garvey and Aikman appealed, at great cost, and the appeal was allowed. So ended the third charge of contempt. Later on a special commission was appointed to probe the affairs of the city council. On the grounds of their finding that body was dissolved.

Unable to do anything for the parishes as he was not in the legislative council, and being hampered in the corporation council in getting his resolution through, Garvey, in June 1930, formed the Workers and Labourers Association.

He led a deputation to the governor, asking him to investigate the distressing conditions of the masses of the island, and to use his influence toward remedial measures. Nonchalantly, the governor replied that in his opinion there was "no unusual suffering." Garvey's next move was to draw up a petition to the kind, through the colonial office. He sent copies to Labour members of Parliament, other liberal-minded men, and newspaper editors in England. The result was the appointment of a royal commission to investigate the political and economic conditions of the West Indies. At the end of September he held a mass meeting in Kingston at Coke Chapel Steps (the outdoor forum) to tell the people the good news.

Mr. J. Denniston, treasurer of the Workers and Labourers Association, presided, and introduced Garvey, who complimented the people on their good behavior during the times of provocation, strain, and misery, and outlined the matters to be brought to the attention of the members of the royal commission.

While a member of the municipality he proposed the following, which was not approved:

> Be it resolved that the Council, for the purpose of carrying out civil improvements, particularly involving better water supply, better lighting installing of proper sewage system, improvement to slum areas, building a Town Hall, erecting new Fire Brigade Station, laying out recreation grounds, and

all such works of magnitude that may be necessary as improvement within the Corporate Area, approach Government for the purpose of securing the necessary authority to float a local loan of five hundred thousand pounds, in order to undertake the carrying out of these improvements immediately.

"Particularly as a means of relieving the present and continuing state of unemployment and hardships among the people. Be it further resolved that the City Engineer be requested to prepare plans and estimates involving the general costs of all these improvements for the guidance of the Council in laying before the Government the manner in which the amount asked for will be spent".

He said that the depression was being felt in the big cities of Europe, England, and the United States of America. Their statements did not ignore it, in fact, they dare not. So with initiative and planning they put into effect measures to alleviate the dole, relief works, feeding of school children, old age pensions, etc.

He declared:

The legislative council instead of tackling our problems at this level ignores them, and continues their individual narrow policy of getting bridges built, a stretch of road repaired, or a water tank erected. Let us set them an example in sensible planning and make the people of Kingston and St. Andrew happy.

Some of us will ask where is the money to come from? It is right here in Jamaica. Just recently I read in the newspapers that a man died and left six hundred and fifty thousand pounds. There are many planters, merchants, and business men who have made their money here, and are wealthy; but alive or dead, they do nothing to benefit the people of their communities. They have no national spirit; but they could be asked to subscribe a loan for development, for which they would be paid interest. This act would also ease their consciences.

The opposing arguments were that such socialist planning had lost the Labour Party an election. They did not intend to assume big responsibilities as they could hardly manage what they had in hand. Put to the vote the motion was lost. It pained Garvey that legislators in both councils refused to legislate for a better Jamaica, from the grassroots up; but he warned them that one day these docile people would rise up in the power of their wrath, and tear down the barriers that keep them, the lower classes, down. The political and economic reforms that he suggested in Jamaica set a pattern for all the other Caribbean territories. He was the pioneer, reformer, and prophet.

# NATIONAL ANTHEM OF THE U.N.I.A.

Ethiopia, thou land of our Father.
The land where the Gods loved to be
As storm clouds at night suddenly gather.
Our armies come rushing to thee.
We must in the fight be victorious,
For us will the victory be glorious;
When led by the Red, Black, and Green.

CHORUS

Advance, advance to victory,
Let Africa be free;
Advance to meet the foe
Advance to meet the foe.
With the might of the Red, the Black,
and Green.
Ethiopia thy tyrant's falling,
Who smote thee upon thy knees.
And thy children are lustly calling
From over the distant seas.

Jehovah the great one has heard us
Has noted our sight and our tears
With his spirit of love he has stirred us
To be one through the coming years.

CHORUS – Advance, Advance, etc.

O Jehovah, Thou God of Ages,
Grant unto our sons that lead
The wisdom thou gave to the sages
When Israel was sore in need.
Thy voice through the dim path has spoken
Ethiopia shall stretch forth her hands
By thee shall all fetters be broken,
And heaven bless our dear Motherland.

# PRAYER

Direct us, O Lord, in all our doings, with
Thy most gracious favor, and further us with Thy continued help;
that in all our works, begun, continued, and ended in Thee, we may
glorify Thy Holy Name, and finally by Thy mercy, obtain
everlasting life; through Jesus Christ, our Lord. Amen.

O God, who has made of one blood, all nations of men that dwell
upon the face of the whole Earth, and didst send Thy Blessed Son
to preach peace and goodwill to all mankind;
grant that men everywhere may seek after Thee and find Thee.
Bring all nations into one fold, and hasten the day of Universal
Brotherhood, through Jesus Christ our Lord. Amen.

Almighty God, whose kingdom is everlasting and power infinite;
be gracious unto the Universal Negro Improvement Association,
and so rule the hearts of Thy servants, The President General, and
members of the high Executive Council, and all others in authority,
that they, knowing the great responsibilities of their office,
may above all things seek the honor and welfare of this race,
and grant that all our people, considering the authoriy they bear,
may faithfully and obediently honor them in accordance with our
laws; through Jesus Chirst, our Lord, who with Thee and the Holy
Ghost, liveth and reigneth ever;
One God, world without end.  Amen.

# Poems by Edith Schamburg

# I AM THE NEGRO

I've known rivers;
I've known rivers ancient as the world
and older than the human blood in human veins.
I bathed in the Euphrates
When dawns were young.
I build my palaces near the Congo.
And it lulled me to sleep.
I looked upon the Nile,
And raised the pyramids above it.
I've known rivers, ancient dusty rivers.
My soul has grown deep, like the rivers.
In the morning of the world
When the fingers of love swept aside the curtains of time
I held the stage
It was I who wooed civilization, and gave birth to nation
Egypt was my first born, and to Us of the Chaldees
I sent my sons and daughters, who scattered empires in Asia
As the wanton winds of Autumn scatter the seeds of flowers.
On the banks of the lazy Nile.
And beside the beautiful Mediterranean
I built great cities whose massive towers kissed the noonday sun.
When only savages roamed the hills of Europe
Mine was a glorious civilization.
Structures of ancient beauty graced my river banks,
Halls of learning and wisdom,
Gorgeously sculptured walls could be seen on every hand,
The wheels of rolling chariots and the tread of marching feet
Were heard upon my stone-paved streets,
States everywhere paid tribute to my conquering hand.
I built Phoenicia, and in ships
With purple sails and gilded galley poles
I sent my children to blue Aegean,
there to found Greece,
The marvel of men and the queen of history.

*Leonard Morris*

Troy was mine and from that burning city fled swarthy Aeneas,
Who set the ferment for Rome, the Eternal City.
My spirit called to Arabia
And out of the Mystic deserts surged the black soldiers of Islam
Who welded the world into a new Empire
And sang their songs of love and victory in the vales of Anealusia.
On the isles of all the ocean,
And from where the southern cross bends low to kiss the restless
waves
To where the Arctic holds in leash its frozen world,
My hand was touched.
Religion, art, literature, science, and civilization are mine.
And eternity but lives in the warmth of my radiant glow,
"I am the Negro."

# BLACK MAN HAD A DREAM

Black man had him a long, deep dream.
He was troubled in mind, dream made it seem
That the voice of a woman, warm and low
was calling him back to a long time ago.
Black man sat up straight in his bed
All kind of nation runnin' 'round in his head.
He called in the air, "Can you hear me, too?
Are you really out there, or am I dreaming of you?"
Your memory stings like the taste of salt.
I left you, I know, but it wasn't my fault.
Its been a long seperation and we didn't keep track.
I've been gone too long now, I can't come back.
Yet, I might come back, but the chance is slim.
I got "a" kind "a" used to the fix I'm in.
I get work all time that you are doing well,
But, for my situtation, it's hard to tell.
Too proud to leave, too proud to stay
And scandalize your name this way.
I'll just stand pat and take in stride
The wretchedness I feel inside.
So mother, Please don't call my name
In dreams. Don't call to mind my shame.
I won't come back. Don't sigh. Don't weep.
Just let me rest. Just let me sleep.
Black Mother's voice come fierce and strong
Son, get up! You 've slept too long.
Night is passing, down is here,
Speeding towards your hemisphere.
My sons at home are in the field
Sowing the power they will yield.
My sons abroad cannot do less
Than match their brohters' manliness.
You can't come back, if you should care.
'Til you have proven manhood there.

25

*Leonard Morris*

My black sons must avenge my rape
Wherever white men found escape!
Stay where you are, and build for me
A corps of black humanity,
Strong independent, back to back.
Proud to be free, proud to be black.
And when I come to my claim,
To settle debts, and clear my name,
My sons wil everywhere, be men.
And then you will come home again.
Black man had him a long, deep dream.
He was troubled in mind, dream made it seem
That as he lay, and dreamed, and slept,
Mother Africa waited, watched, and wept.

# A PEEP AT PAST

If others laugh at you, return the laughter to them; if they mimic you, return the compliment with equal force. They have no more right to dishonor, disrespect, and disregard your feelings and manhood than you have in dealing with them. Honor them when they honor you; disrespect and disregard them when they vilely treat you. Their arrogance is but skin deep and an assumption that has no foundation in morals or in law. They have sprung from the same family tree of obscurity as we have; their history is as rude in its primitiveness as ours; their ancestors ran wild and naked, lived in caves and in branches of trees, like monkeys as ours; they made human sacrifices, ate the flesh of their own dead, and the raw meat of the wild beast for centuries even as they accuse us of doing; their cannibalism was more prolonged than ours; when we were embracing the arts and sciences on the banks of the Nile; their ancestors were still drinking human blood and eating out of the skulls of their conquered dead. When our civilization had reached the noonday of progress, they were still running naked and sleeping in holes and caves with rats, bats, and other insects and animals. After we had already unfathomed the mystery of the stars and reduced the heavenly constellations to minutes and regular calculus, they were still backwoodsmen, living in ignorance and blatant darkness.

*Leonard Morris*

# <u>ALLEGIANCE TO SELF FIRST</u>

Let no voice but your own speak to you from the depths. Let no influence but your own rouse you in time of peace and war. Hear all, but attend only to that which concerns you. Your allegiance shall be to your God, then to your family, race and country. Remember always that the Jew in his political and economic urge is always first a Jew, the white man is first a white man under all circumstances, and you can do no less than being first and always a Negro, and then all else will take care of itself. Let no man innoculate you with evil doctrines to suit their own conveniences. There is no humanity before that which starts with yourself. "Charity begins at home." First to thyself be true, and thou canst not then be false to any man.

# Poems by Marcus Garvey

*Leonard Morris*

# EMPTY DREAMS

You will see that from the start
we tried to dignify our race.
If I am to condemned for
that I am satisfied.

# DAYS OF DECLINE

All of us may not live to see
the higher accomplishment of
an African empire, so strong
and powerful, as to compel the
respect of mankind, but we in
our lifetime can so work and
act as to make the dream a
possibility within another
generation.

*Leonard Morris*

# **<u>BE PROUD</u>**

Each race should be proud and
stick to its own,
And the best of what they are
should be shown.
This is no shallow song of hate
to sing.
But over black there should be no
white king.
Every man of his own foothold
should stand.
Claiming a nation and a fatherland.
White, Yellow, and Black should
make their own laws,
And force no one-sided justice
with flaws.

## <u>ONE AIM, ONE GOD, ONE DESTINY</u>

Be as proud of your race today as our father
within the days of yore.
We have a beautiful history, and we shall
create another in the future that will astonish
the world.

*Leonard Morris*

# **<u>A SON IS GIVEN</u>**

I know no national boundary
where the Negro is concerned.
The whole world is my
province until Africa is free.

# UP, YOU MIGHTY RACE

Now we have started to speak,
and I am only the forerunner
of an awakened Africa that shall
never go back to sleep.

*Leonard Morris*

# <u>A RACE</u>

A race without authority and
power is a race without respect.

# Poems by Leonard Morris

*Leonard Morris*

# **THE ARTIST**

The substance of man is such that he has
to satisfy the needs of life with
all his senses.

His very being cries out for these senses
to appropriate the true riches of
life, the beauty of human relationships,
and the dignity of nature and art,
realized in striving toward a bright
tomorrow…

Without a history,
a culture, without creative art
inspiring these senses, mankind
stumbles in a chasm of despair
and pessimism.

My work takes shape around images
and ideas that are centered within the
vortex of a black experience,
A nitty-gritty ghetto experience
resulting in contraditory emotions,
Anguish, hope, love, despair, happiness,
faith, lack-of-faith, dreams.
Stubbornly holding on to an elusive
romantic belief that the people of
this land cannot always be insensible to the
dictates of justice or deaf to the voice of humanity.

## <u>CONFIDENCE</u>

If God is with you
there should be no problem.
Remember He speaks to you,
through your inner self.
So apply yourself to it.

*Leonard Morris*

# AFRICAN FUNDAMENTALISM

The time has come for the Negro to forget and cast behind him his hero worship and adoration of other races, and so start out immediately to create and emulate heroes of his own. We must recognize our own saints and martyrs and elevate to positions of fame and honor black men and women who have made their distinct contributions to our racial history.

Africa has produced a countless number of men and women in war and in peace, whose luster and bravery outshine that of any other people. Then why not see good and perfection in ourselves? We must inspire a literature and promulgate a doctrine of our own without any apologies to the powers that be. The right is ours and God's. Let contrary sentiment and cross opinions go by the winds.

Opposition to race independence is the weapon of the enemy to defeat the hopes of an unfortunate people. We are entitled to our own opinions and not obligated to or bound by the opinions of others.

# Poems by Leonard Morris

*Leonard Morris*

# <u>LOVE</u>

O love, you have
comforted me,
what would I do
without you.
Now that you are here,
stay, stay and never turn away.

# **<u>TRUST</u>**

Will thou be faithful
and will our path be clear?
Though in the dark,
henceforth there will be light.
Twilight is down,
I rest in peace
for the morning to come.

*Leonard Morris*

# **<u>AMBITION</u>**

Position is gained
by ability,
Ability is gained from
hard work by experience
and perseverance
That's the only Ambition
one could aim for,
to be successful.

## <u>HAPPINESS</u>

In liking what
you do
is the secret of happiness.

# THE ARTIST

I am a creative person,
endeavoring to communicate
and express myself
via fine arts.
I have always been
in the minority far afield
of the mainstream of our society.
I have to cope with special
problems, the main problem
being rejection.  Many times
the frustration I have to
encounter is overwhelming, and
I would withdraw, plotting a course
of mutual rejection as a solution to
my particular problems.  When
this happens, the only thing
I am left with is my work.
Putting myself out of touch in
this manner, then my work begins
to suffer, causing deeper
frustration resulting in more
severe psychological problems.
Humble as I, a painter,
reaching out for mankind,
desire FAME and WEALTH.
Only success, I can assure,
is hard work and be myself.
Master your work by
doing it your way.
And it shall be said,
he did it his way.

# <u>**OBSTACLE**</u>

I will not quit,
inspite of obstacles.
I know I will overcome
my dreams.
Once I have done it
then my soul can rest in peace.
Then mankind will surely smile at
my achievements.

*Leonard Morris*

# <u>TWO KINDS OF PEOPLE</u>

There are two kinds of people on earth
today,
Just two kinds of people, no more,
I say,
Not the good and the bad for 'tis
well understood
The good and half bad and the bad are half
good.
Not the humble and proud, for in life's
busy span
Who puts on vain airs is not counted a man.
No, the two kinds of people on earth I mean,
Are the people who lift and the people
who lean
Wherever you go, you will find the world's
masses
Are ever divided in just these two
classes.
And strangely enough you will.

## <u>LIFE</u>

Live the life you love
love the life you live,
Life is what you make it to be.


In liking what you do,
is the secret of happiness.

# <u>WOMEN</u>

She can be good and she can be bad,
If she wants to be good, she can
be good, and if she wants to be bad,
she can be bad.
One only has to hope for the best,
THE GOOD.

# THE WIND

The wind is blowing,
We listen to the sound.
The mind is alert,
The body is prepared,
My, my, I have got an idea.

*Leonard Morris*

# <u>HAPPINESS</u>

Happiness is like a butterfly,
The more you chase it, the more
it will elude you,
But if you put your attention
to other things,
It comes and softly sits on
your shoulder.

# <u>WHERE AM I</u>

Where am I going?
Can't you show me the way?
Hence my thoughts go astray.
When thou art with me,
my troubles are over.
Beyond the perspective,
lies my dream of dreams.
To be what I ought to be
is to work toward the goal.
Thou shall not turn thy back
from the dream you thought of.
Go toward the perspective
And never be discouraged.

*Leonard Morris*

# THE MOON

Thou desire to go on the moon,
while man is making pathway,
for a new dream,
but thou have a long way to go.
Why leave the poor to suffer.
There is no such thing as one
to live on the moon.
Don't kill mankind, he needs to live on.
Just say I was on the moon for the
knowledge of mankind
and leave others ALONE.

# <u>MY FAMILY</u>

My family I love.
Without them, life wouldn't
be worthwhile.
They are my future,
who thou rest thy thoughts within,
Be he what I shouldn't or can't
my children will be.
My confidence lies with my wife,
with assurance of trustfulness.
From these phrases will make,
thee a better Artist for mankind.

*Leonard Morris*

# <u>ETIQUETTE</u>

The nicest things people
can say to each other,
Good Morning, Pardon Me,
Good Night, Thank You.
Thus these Etiquettes
bring out the true
quality of a person.

# <u>HI, DEAR</u>

Where art thou?
when thou wandered.
Thou search and find not.
I trust thy wind will do his part,
in bringing you on the
right pathway.
So wander not, for ye
art in your direction.
Tho to my surprise,
around the corner, a
voice says, Hi!  Dear.

*Leonard Morris*

# **<u>PROBLEMS</u>**

You never know one's troubles.
Altho he never says,
But who cares.
Tho the unseen spirit knows it.
You would rather say it to him,
If your mind isn't sure.
Comfort your soul,
by telling your troubles,
to someone close to you.

# I CAME FROM THE NIGGER YARD

I come from the nigger yard of yesterday
Leaping from the oppressors hate and score of myself
from the agony of the dark hut in the shadow and the hurt
of thing, from the long days of cruelty and the long nights
of pain
Down to the wide streets of tomorrow, of the next day
Leaping I come, who cannot see will hear.
In the nigger yard I was naked like the new born
Naked like a stone or a star.

It was a cradle of blind days racking in time
Torn like the skin from the back of a slave.
It was an aching floor on which I crept
On my hands and my knees searching the dust for the trace
of a roof

Or the mark of a leaf or the shape of a flower
It was me always walking with bare feet,
Meeting strange faces like those dreams of fever.
When the whole world turns upside down
And no one knows which is the sky or the land
which heart is this among the strange and terible walking
about groaning between the wind.

And there was always sad music somewhere in the land
like a bugle and a drum between the houses;
Voices of women singing far away
Pauses of silence, then a flood of sound,
But these were things like ghosts or spirits of wind.
It was only a big world spinning outside
And men born in agony, torn in torture, twisted and stained
and sordid…

Like the world big and cruel, spinning outside
Sitting sometimes in the twilight near the forest
Where all the light is gone and every bird
I notice is a tiny star neighboring a leaf
A little drop of light, a piece of glass

Straining over heaven tiny bright
Like a spark seed in the destiny of gloom
Oh it was the heart like this tiny star near to the sorrows
Staining against the whole world and the long turn of light
Spark of man's dream conquering the night
Moving in darkness stubborn and fierce
Till leaves of sunset change from green to blue
And shadows grow like giants everywhere.
So, was I born again stubborn and fierce screaming
in a slum.
It was a city and a coffin space for home
A river running prison, hospitals,
Men drunk and dying, judges full of scorn
Priests, and parsons fooling gods with words
And me, like a dog tangled in rags
Spotted with sores powdered with dust
Screaming with hunger, any or with life and men.
It was a child born from a mother full of her blood
Weaving has features bleeding her of her blood life clots.
It was pain lasting from to months and to years
Weaving a pattern telling a tale leaving a mark
On the face and brow.
Until there came the oven days cast in a foundry
And flying it in the face of those who hate me
It is me the nigger boy turning to manhood
Linking my fingers, welding my flesh to freedom.

## <u>DO IT</u>

Why do you pretend,
you're only making thyself
a fool.
Wake up out of those
stupid ways, and let
yourself go, and do
your thing.

**Vendors**

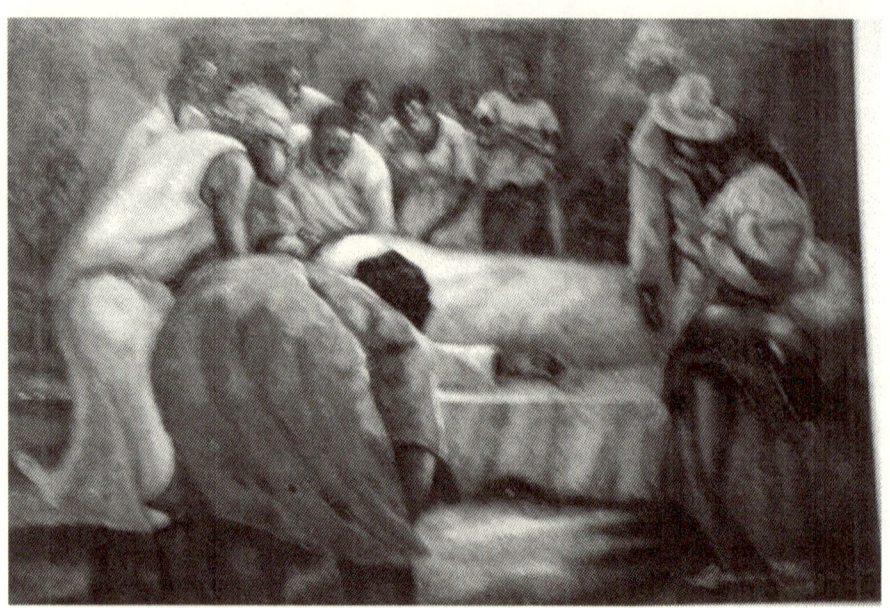

**Death of Marcus Garvey**

**African Woman**

**Out of many, one people**

**Mandela and his first wife**

*Leonard Morris*

**Black struggle**

**Garvey's Court Trial**

**Harlem Float**

**Black Vibes**

**Tide**

**Inspiration**

**Heritage**

**Injustice**

**Transportation**

**The Subway Arrest**

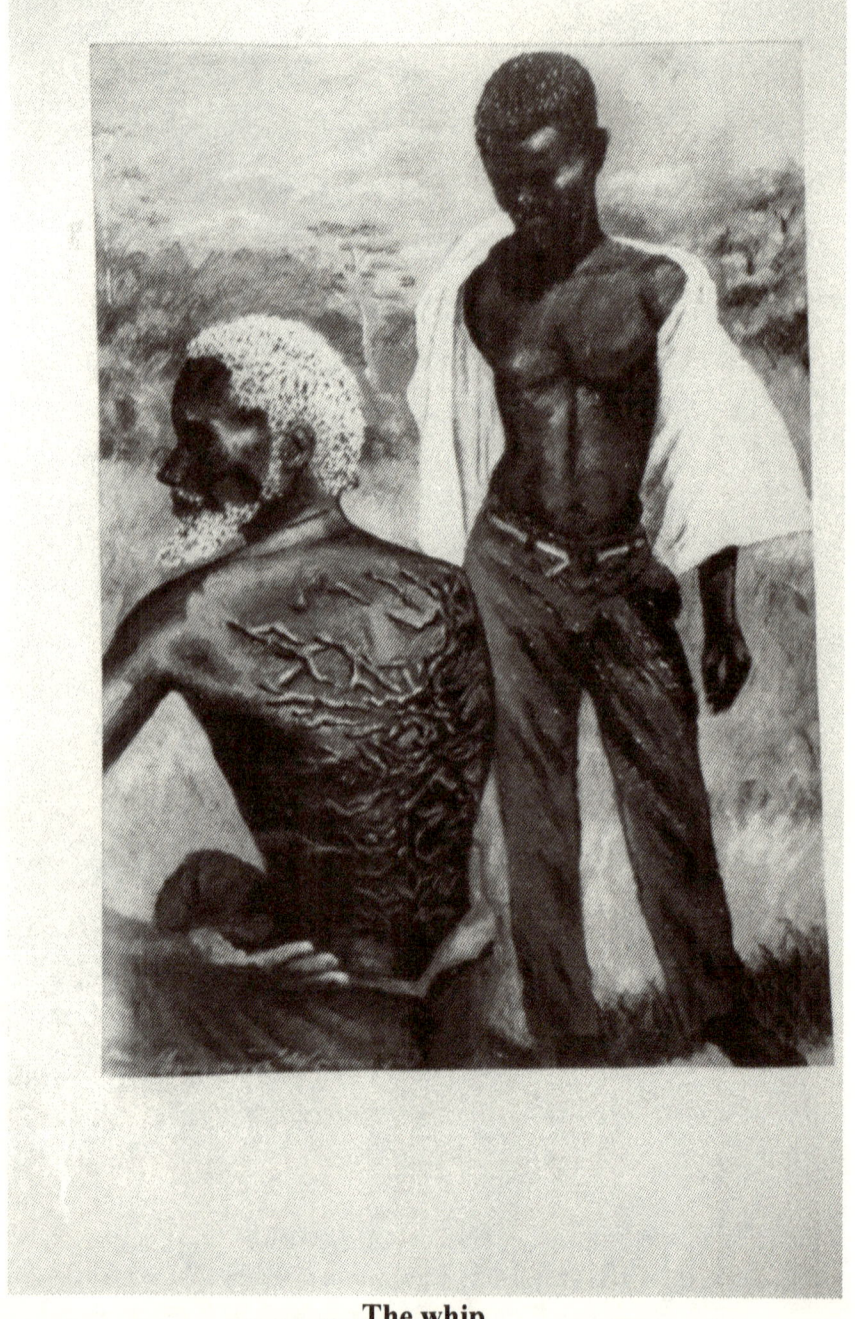

**The whip**

**Family Re-union**

**Marcus Garvey in Jail**

**Marcus Garvey's Birth home**

**Carnival**

**Street Corner Meeting**

**Inspecting the Guards**

**Members of the African Region on parade in New York**

**Group of Juveniles in Convention Parade**

**Learning to Read**

**U. N. I. A. Shares**

**U. N. I. A. Nurses**

**Garvey's Deportation from U. S. A.**

**Garvey's doctor in England**

**Garvey's First Wife Amy Ashwood Garvey, which he divorced.**

**Going to school**

**Steaming Court Trial**

**The K. K. K. Treat**

**Booker T. Washington**

**Garvey at the age of 12 years with his neighbor**

**Nursing Aids**

**Dr. W. E. B. Dubois**

**Garvey's Papers, "Negro World"**

**Dr. Julius Garvey**

**Professor Marcus Garvey Jr.**

**Young Mrs. Garvey**

**The Auxiliaries**

# LEONARD FRANKLIN MORRIS:  A PROFILE
## *Impressionist, Portraitist, Muralist and Multifaceted Composition Specialist Painter*

**LEONARD FRANKLIN MORRIS**, an Impressionist, Portraitist, Muralist and multifaceted Composition Specialist, was born in Jamaica, West Indies, on September 14, 1932, to late Eva Hutchinson and Desmond Morris.  He is a graduate of Knox College and the Jamaica School of Art. He also attended Kingston Technical High School where he studied Woodwork.  In 1947, at age 14, Morris sold his first painting entitled *"Country Man"* to the British Consulate.

Morris read art books and did pencil sketches at the Junior Center Library of the Institute of Jamaica.  The director of the center, Bob Verity, saw his work and promptly sent him to join the Vera Cummings art class where he studied painting alongside such artists as Barrington Watson, Corah Hamilton, Vernal Reuben, David Pottinger, Osmond Watson, Alexander Cooper and the late master painter and printmaker Lloyd van-Pitterson.  Morris also studied sculpture under the late master sculptor Alvin Marriott, ceramics under master potter Cecil Baugh and printing under the master printer E. C. R. Williams.

In 1952 Morris won a scholarship to the Jamaica School of Art and Crafts where he studied drawing, painting and graphic art.  Morris spent seven years studying under the tutelage of the late painter Karl Parboosingh, Ralph Campbell, and the late painter and master sculptor Edna Manley. He later served as Artist-In-Residence at the University of the West Indies and Knox College.  Morris' long-term goal was to win a scholarship to go to England where he hoped to master the various techniques to become an art teacher so he could devote his life to teaching drawing and painting.  This did not happen.  Morris accepted a job with the Jamaica Telephone Director Service as their art director for two years. He then moved on to Jerry Dunlop Associates as they layout artist.  He also worked with NACK Advertising Associates as their finish artist; with Eddie Williams Associate as Assistant Art Director, and Foster Advertising as their Finish Artist. Wishing to continue doing fine art, in 1968 Morris migrated to the United States in search of great opportunities.

In 1968, he migrated to the U.S.A. in search of greater opportunities. At the Art Student League of New York, he assisted the late Professor Charles Alston with his students. Then he attended the Washington Art School in the District of Columbia in Washington, D.C., for two years. He studied under the late master painter Hector Whistler. Morris returned to Jamaica to open his own studio at the Institute of Jamaica. He was nominated in 1952 as *Artist of the Year* at the Annual Art Exhibition in Jamaica. In 1955 his oil painting "*Country Dance*" gained him honorable mention in the Jamaica Art Competition. In 1965 he was awarded merits in the Jamaica Art Competition. A year later he was honored at the Canadian Art Exposition.

In 1971 works by Morris were selected to represent Jamaica in the Commonwealth Arts Exposition in London, England. In 1952, his artwork "*Grief*" received rave reviews from the late renowned British Play writer Noel Coward who told him that, "*Grief is the best piece of artwork*" he had seen outside of Europe. The piece was purchased by the Institute of Jamaica. In 1997, his painting "*Out of Many One People*" caught the eye of Mayor Rudolph Giulliani in 1997. The Mayor's laudatory comments were, "*this painting is an excellent image of the ethnic diversity which makes up New York City*."

Over the years Morris' works have achieved international recognition and have won numerous awards. He is the only artist who has created a body of work in oil, watercolors and pen sketches chronicling the "*Life and times of the late Jamaican National Hero, the Hon. Marcus Mossiah Garvey*." The 80 pieces in the collection document Garvey's birth, the house in which he was born, his arrest by the FBI on a train on 125th Street, up to his death. Morris recently produced another series entitled "*Cricket*" consisting of images of famous cricketers.

Morris has been exhibited his works in group and one-man exhibitions in galleries, churches, offices and homes in England, West Germany, Jamaica, Canada, Cuba, Puerto Rico and the United States. He is listed in the Director of Caribbean Personalities in Britain and North America, and "**Who's Who In America in Black Arts**." He has been featured in numerous newspaper and magazine articles and on TV and radio programs, his works can be found in many prominent private collections.

## ARTIST'S STATEMENT:

"My work takes shape around images and ideas that focus on the Black Experience. That is why I painted the Marcus Garvey series to symbolize the vast contributions that one man made to the race to keep his dream alive."

## PERSONAL:

Morris resides in St. Albans, New York, with his wife Victoria (Pauline) Bailey. He has one sister and a brother who is deceased. He is the father of two sons Christopher and Michael. He has six grandchildren: Gianna, Ebony, Justine, Joshua, Faith and Kenya. He is a devoted member of the Bronx Baptist Church and an ordained Deacon. He has retired from his many years of service in the health care profession. Morris spends his time painting, writing poetry and articles for this Church Bulletin, and administering to the needy.